American Falls

American Falls

Poems by
Greg Keeler

A James R. Hepworth Book

Confluence Press, Inc. / 1987

Acknowledgements

Thanks to the editors of the following publications which first printed some of these poems: *The Affinitive Angler, The Berkeley Poetry Review, Connecticut Quarterly, Corona, Cutbank, English Journal, Gray's Sporting Journal, Montana Review, The Montana Trout Unlimited Bulletin, Northern Lights, Plains Poetry Journal, The Prairie Schooner, River Styx, Salt Cedar, The Slackwater Review, Strong Measures: Contemporary American Poetry in Traditional Forms, Tales from Gray's, Tar River Poetry, Trestle Creek Review,* and *Wetting our Lines Together* (an anthology of American fishing poetry published by Tamarack Press).

I would like to gratefully acknowledge the editorial assistance of Keith and Shirley Browning, Jim Hepworth, and Robert Wrigley who are responsible for publishing many of these poems in my first two limited editions, *Spring Catch* and *The Far Bank*, through Confluence Press.

My thanks also to Ken Cook, Brad Donovan, and Mary Rohrberger for their suggestions and support and Paul Ferlazzo and Karen Swenson who got me started publishing books.

Copyright © 1987 by Greg Keeler

ISBN 0-917652-63-0
LIBRARY OF CONGRESS CARD NUMBER 87-47733

Publication of this book is made possible by grants from the Idaho Commission on the Arts, a State agency, and the National Endowment for the Arts in Washington, D.C., a Federal agency.

Ilustrations by Greg Keeler

Typesetting and Production by
Susan Lundvall and Jane Stellyes.
Cover Design by Andrew A. Caldwell and Susan Lundvall

Published by

Confluence Press, Inc.
Lewis Clark State College
8th Avenue & 6th Street
Lewiston, Idaho 83501

Distributed to the trade by

Kampmann & Company
9 East 40th Street
New York, New York 10016

In memory of Clinton Keeler
1919-1979

A blackbird with red
shoulders squee-gees.

A catfish with a moonlight
belly and a back as green
as winter wheat
moves in channel or pool
to take a hopper worm
or doughbait.

Lacking those
he glides toward the cool
gunnysack of any kid
under fifteen
who doesn't know

he's not a blackbird.

           —Clinton Keeler, *Prelapsarian*

CONTENTS

AMERICAN FALLS

PSALMS, ODES, AND RANTS

DRIVING THE BLIZZARD

NEAR MYTHS

SPRING CATCH

I'm going to be a child about it and I can't help it, I was
born this way and it makes me very happy to fish and drink.

—Jim Harrison, *Drinking Song*

FOR THE TROUT
I
Cutthroat

You were here first.
I can see why in
the way the rivers don't
rob you of what the streams gave.

The dim rosettes on your
sides live behind your spots
in another time
as if Lewis and Clark were
still planning to meet near
water and would never stop.

And the thin orange slashes
on your throat will always
be proof. No matter how
the world may crowd toward
the hybrid of loss
they will be there.

Your gill covers burn crimson
toward purple as you flaunt
the purity of the West
spilling east from the divide
and a world
lost in you.

II
Brook

You live hard
in the backwaters and eddies
where your flesh turns
like coal into diamond
and you burn orange
up the flare of your fins
for your own reason.

The tracks stunning your
back into dark marble
are where we would go in
sleep if dream were water.
Since it's not we rely on
you to show us the way east.

When you find size
in still waters, four pounds
draped over a purist's hand,
it leaves no choice:
Plato was wrong.
All of the West was wrong.
This living shadow burns,
has weight.

III
Brown

You have come a
long way—and stayed.
Still you seem willing to put
up with us.

When we take your water away,
slow it down,
turn it warm,
your jaw gets more determined
with each fall spawning—
and you grow.

We call you brown and your
red spots defy us, floating
on brown glowing gold
turning purple or turquoise
when you flop on the grass.

Your teeth turn inward
sharp down your throat
so nothing you catch
can escape you.

IV
Rainbow

Running against the
line you are the
promise. Where the
brown dives, you leap.
And there in the sun,
above the circle of
your entrance into
this world,
you let us know for
one instant what
you know. And there
is nothing in
the color of sun through
water that could spell
promise so clearly.

On shore your colors
go quickest of all.
Unless we lose you now
we will lose you always.

THE GLASS TROUT

It lies over the rocks.
Or at least its shadow does.
It turns to feed.
Or at least its refraction does.

Here is a bright window
on a world where
everything is clear
until it moves
and everything moves.

A nose breaks the surface
in a circle small as
a bracelet for a slender wrist
but the shadow beneath
cannot even hide behind a boulder
so it moves up and back
under the hatch.

It is a rock
then a weed bed
then a sunstruck wave.

Then it arches out into
this world
where everthing stops.

PANFISH

If you can't figure it out,
name it after the way you eat it.
Sunfish hovered in clumps
over the circles of their
pebble beds. We jerked them up
like turnips and only stopped
briefly to hold them slab flat
on our palms—to look into
bright colors the air can't keep.
Once under a frozen lake, yellow
perch drifted in clouds
the size of Buicks. We stood above
them shuddering in long underwear,
stacking them beside us and
filleting them late into
the northern night. We drifted
our minnows through midwestern
reservoirs, and the crappie came,
slapping the moonlight to ribbons.
I've returned grinning from
these flesh gluts, my fingers
crisp with scales, my dreams
full of lost gloves, swimming
from closet corners,
thumbs up like dorsals,
ready to shake hands.

SPRING CATCH

We drove far up into the canyon
from the sunny plain to a day
of light cold drizzle. When
we finally got to the bridge, gray

snow, new and melting had stained
the river brown. Beyond a foot
deep, the rocks blurred and rain
distorted those we could see. I put

on my waders and two men in a truck
pulled up. "There's a body somewhere
between here and Karst Ranch; with luck
you might snag it. They found the other near

where the boat turned over." In winding
gears and peeled up mist the yellow
truck turned gray and was gone. Things
weren't the same after that, though

the rain kept its superficial patterns
and the fishing was good. The huge
pool, my favorite hole, had new stones
as with every cast my line lodged

where it never had before, and when
I tried to free it, something reminded
me of my own hand
at the other end of the line.

SALMON FLY HATCH ON YANKEE JIM CANYON OF THE YELLOWSTONE

First the bank-grass sags black,
heavy with climbing. A few
fat cruisers sucked into slate
swirls mark a beginning that builds
high to the cliffs. You stand
by your car at a turnoff
and your hair fills with them:
Pteronarcys, horror on wings,
bodies long as penknives.
There is no bite, just
the cool abdomens dragging on skin
then mounting the evening breeze
in squadrons, black helicopters
whirring away from what you would have
them be. The sky is dark then
clear and the range of the
river's huge swirl swirls
in miniature a thousand times.
This life wrings itself under its
wings into the life of the waves.
Each salmon-orange speck spells
its name on black and pronounces
itself as new flesh of the same
color in each slick nose nudging
it down. As the sun goes so do
these. In the click of a car
door, you're on toward a job,
a family, a lover—sucked into
the current of the highway
where oncoming cars dim their
lights to small specks
swirling the distance into
a thousand places,
and each will be home.

BLACK BASS SCHOOL:
TOLEDO BEND RESERVOIR,
LOUISIANA

A storm's coming and the sky
rolls blue-black over the half-
sunken forest.
Behind it the sun burns red
and here over the boat, somewhere
between. Now the water is still
but choppy in the distance. It
is the school, chasing shad,
flashing their black spots like
eyes to the side then nothing.
The mirage of wind moves closer
until we hear it, snapping
and popping toward us, toward
the storm. The grotesque lures
we throw, stare at us over
their metal bills.
The storms converge
at our boat and we throw
to feel the electricity
coming to our rods from one,
to the water from the other.
Our boat lies in the boil
as we handle fish after fish,
sag-bellied, black holes for mouths.
The rain beats us silly
and it should. We're part of it.
It slaps us back like these
fins on water until we know
we've lost and run for it.

STONEFLIES

Today stoneflies covered
the stones, my clothes,
my neck; and whitefish
broke the slack seams
of the Gallatin as if

the spring snowed black
against winter and boiled
the water white to
turquoise currents.
This before the Bridgers'

snow came clear
up against the sky,
sealing horizons tight
to keep me whistling
back at spring creeks

coming in at me
and brushing away new skins
buzzing light on my skin
until the sun burned
the current into my

new color darkening
as the flecked rocks
below and above,
the sky, blue down
its farthest wave.

BROOK TROUT
BEHIND A BEAVER DAM

Chewed ends of willow
and gold bark are the only
bright marker where water
stops clear on pebbles.
But pluck a rosehip
from the bush behind you,
and where you toss it,
gills flare like swallows
turning in the wind.
Red flashes near a belly
so orange the black
and white slashes become
the whole fall,
wrinkled there
under the water's small breaking.
When you look up the deep-cut
meandering of this meadow
with its sharp new rust,
up the foothills,
spattered yellow with aspen,
up the timberline
fading to new snow and
the blue, blown full
as your lungs of the hot-cold
air; massive clouds swim
the wind, flared gold at the edges,
sucking the sun in
and blowing it out.

GETTING MINNOWS

A hot day is cool under awnings.
The man who runs this place moves
slowly, cool too as his fingers
skim dead shiners from the surface
where the hiss of bubbles sends
them swirling and belly up. He
knows there is nothing urgent on
these afternoons; his overalls stay
crisp in the smell of small fish
dead. Now he has the net with the
broad head and slides it deep against
concrete. Skirting the corners
then flipping it up quick, he lays
the frame across the tank rim so
the net bags and boils silver. With
a smaller net he counts them out;
then, to let you know how involved
he is, he tosses in a rough fist-
full extra. Stepping back from
the awnings, you laugh to yourself
at the bright red and white sign:
SHINNERS. And he laughs too as
you walk to your car with the
absurd little bucket at your side.

LENNIGAR'S LAKE

At Lennigar's lake we'd duck
through the grass; if he saw us
he'd always run us off. If we stayed
our cheap fly rods played hell
with the bluegill. Ticks got us
bad once when we waded near redbud
in bloom, and once when a channel cat
the size of a dog wobbled out of
cattail shallows, I followed and stepped
on some tin, clouding the water.
Up the bank scorpions curled in the
hollows of logs, and centipedes like African
bracelets clicked under rocks we'd
turn up looking for worms.
We burned ourselves purple, wading
those summers into the day they
drained the lake. People who lived
in the red hills around came with
dynamite and a boat: the old men in
blue and pink Sunday shirts and
the women in bonnets 'til the boat
rode high on the blast in the last pool.
Clods from the bottom blew over oaks
pelting pinics and scabbing
the heads of boys in the open.
By evening a line of deep bellied bass
and catfish dried on the grass.

AFTER THE HATCH
(Gallatin Gateway, Montana)

They told me the hatch was on
up the canyon, that they had to use
their wipers driving through the dark
cloud until spattered with ooze.
When I drove up it was gone;
Sofa Pillows, Bitch Creeks, nothing worked

but the rain, lining fog and pines,
soaking me to a pucker under my poncho.
Bright sod tops of the undercut sank
and left me tired and standing. When branches
of alder caught me I grabbed. A fine
flurry of husks swirled up the bank,

riding the air and loose waves
in the same direction. These are my
hatch, my only way out of this stiff spring,
a distorted spiral cramped by wind to sky,
by current to all the brittle graves
of an old life that was bent
on being wings for the new.

BOZEMAN CREEK

I glimpse you from the window, striding towards the river.

When you return, reeking of fish and beer,
There is salt dew in your hair. Where have you been?
Your clothes weren't that wrinkled hours ago, when you left.

—Carolyn Kizer, *Summer Near The River*

THE SMALL STREAM

When the rivers are too much,
when the wide stretches and far banks
leave me nonplussed at such
depths, rocks, beds of weed, I give thanks

for the small streams: those I can
straddle and see the deep pools clear
to the bottom. They are worth the fan
of wet leaves, the tangle of willow, alder

the sting of rosehip. The fish are always
smaller but their colors more intense,
just as the will to survive a small space
whets them down to an edge of pure sense.

If the shadow of a bird shoots across
my fly, I jerk. If a quick trout passes,
I look up. And if my fly gets lost
in an inch thin riffle, an inch thick hiss

of trout is there flashing and diving into
nearly nothing. Yeats thought he was romantic,
but he probably forgot about looking through
water at the roots of trees, the alembic

of a deep pool, at such a pure
concentration of light. And when he laid
it on his cabin floor,
he could easily have seen that maid

with apple blossoms in her hair,
for in the deep rocks, rosehips and water between,
I can still get lost in colors, but there
is no magic in a small stream.

POOL ON THE GALLATIN

I
Head

The gravel tongue flickers
under water humps, small
then large to rocks.
Through the speed of current
quartz, flint, granite
shine with the deep greens,
reds and yellows of wet fruit.
Flip a flat rock and flat nymphs
hug and scuttle to the top
turned bottom, or twirl off
in tandem to the drop turned aqua.

II
Riffle

Here, nothing is clear but
water diced 'till rock
is fish and fish
is sun turned solid.
Turning to feed, twisted
in a glint where a seam
divides what you can see
into blues the sky threw back,
trout hug the sides of water-speed.

III
Hole

Stillness fixes itself in
cobalt over mud. Everything
is obvious yet vacant.
A log works its way into silt.
At the edges, roll a large
rock and sculpins wobble
flat heads, bat fins into the
bottom's gauze.

IV
Run

The current is launched in
its swing from the far bank
and kids you with a poker face.
Alder roots tickle the rocks
you can't see and avoid those
you can. In spite of it, this
is what a river should be:
fast, direct, reflecting clouds.

V
Tail

Now it shallows out
wide and smooth. Whitefish
break the mirror lightly with
lip and tail. In a slight twist
whole schools drift sideways
and flash over yellow stones.

MADISON CADDIS

Old Rosehip berries, puckered
to russet, bent
on the lowest branches,
almost to the river's hiss,
are hidden in this new crop,
flocked out powder brown.
Lace wings up close flutter
the river-light
then far back these gleams
are rainbows rising
near shadows.
Foothills from Bear Trap Canyon
green the new life
out of clouds, patterning
whole worlds of darkness
across the broad valley.
Fresh wind and light
came between the rain
all day, until now
when it stops
here above the surface
tension, catching the brief sun.
They drift like glowing seeds
to be planted in those
quavering pops and circles
there, there, there, and there.

VEGAS ON THE JEFFERSON

Slots ring in light
and water through logjams.
The sun's a blonde
keno runner I can't keep
from watching,
but who's counting cards?

Two otters,
drunk on a ripped-up trout,
fight it out
along cottonwood
downed on a riffle.

Where light hits wave,
stoneflies get rich
but pump it right back
into the river.

Nobody here will ever win
enough. The Bitch Creek
I'm using looks neon,
as if it were dreamed up
late in a woozy blue lounge.
It's a billboard flashing
            EAT
down silt and stone.
A three pound brown does.
A few bats take the moon
to the door and cash it in.

NIGHT WALK
ON THE WEST BOULDER RIVER

Walking down a gravel road
that traces the seam of the
West Boulder, you see no moon,
just stars and a small animal
following you each time you
turn around. It's not a dog
or cat and it's not large enough
to hurt you or to out-run you,
but still it's there as it
would never be in the daylight.
A deer breaks from the
tall grass toward the river
and you jump, perhaps even make
a small noise, but it's still
there ten yards behind you.
You turn around and stop
and it stops. Its eyes don't
glow. It might as well not
have eyes, so you walk faster,
your camp a dark spot buried
in pines by a bend in the river
waiting for you like you wait
for that thought to come and
bring back last night's dream.
And when it does, you turn
around and that small persistant
ball of darkness is gone,
leaving its absence as large
as the new sound of the river
is close.

BOZEMAN CREEK

It starts up in the Hyalites
where elk dab their
tongues and runs quick on rocks
down through farms sparse then
thick to developments
then town. All of this in ten
miles packs history to an instant
lesson where the pupils are awed
by the teacher's knowledge but
never learn.

The fast water moves to undercut
meadows to parks then beneath
pavement, buildings, old houses,
railroad tracks, then out to join
the slower streams and rivers
rip-rapped with broken concrete
and old cars.

In town the law leaves fishing
to the children, so they learn best.
One might drift a worm under
the tire store, the Eagles Bar,
the bank parking lot, the old hotel
and catch brook trout: pale, thin
memories of cutthroats that
lie upstream or prophesies of survival
in rough German browns that burrow
downstream in the carcasses
of rusted out cars.

One spring the stream took
a girl fresh from drink at the Eagles
and pulled her under downtown Bozeman
in the range of those dim brook trout.

It is spring again and the water
comes cold, hard and fast
from where the elk dips
to where these ghosts hold firm
in the current under the old hotel.

BOZEMAN PONDS

Next to the shopping mall
the ponds reflect willows and
street lamps. A government
truck filled them with six pound
trout. Foot broken, I drive
the parking lot to the edge
and hop down among plastic
cups and burger cartons.
I prop my foot up on an oil can
and watch my bobber.

Melted in the hot car yesterday,
the worms are hell to get on the hook.
I top off the gob with a piece of corn.

The bobber's under but I see
a woman on the other bank
in a puce bikini instead.

A dog swims over my line.

Soon I have two rainbows:
their fins almost gone
from battling hatchery tanks,
their will no match
for my cheap reel. The woman
in the bikini stands up to watch.
Snuffling the water
another dog swims by.

THE FAR BANK

Whitefish are rising.
I know the way their tails
take the moon. I'd say
I'm wasted, stripping this
Muddler in at twelve a.m.,
but there is something
near the far bank
making its arc gleam
on the roar. I think
no moon could flash
that bright once removed.
It's lived here nosing
the evening hatches summers,
tearing up the shallows
for sculpin at night.
I've come to face it again,
to hear its wallow and
feel it bump my line.
And then I'll leave to tell
this over and over to you
whose moon is stitched
with late hatches to a life
that keeps breaking
in imperfect rings.
Our gear rattles on us
and we stumble on slick
boulders as if we were
chained to this river
that calls its own name
later and louder every night.

EAST GALLATIN

Bodies of rusted cars hold
back the banks, and water
gluts the windows. Filled
with stonefly larvae, trout are

living where someone's uncle
probably sat with no air-
conditioning, a light tickle
of vent wind drumming summer

past his eyes wrinkled to West-
Montana sun on sun and mountain.
I'm riding with him now and the rest
of this river stretch, counting

car bodies and their trout psyches,
deep in seat springs behind old
six-volt batteries charged with algae
and still travelling this darker road.

I feel the old air too, waders sucked
in river silt that used to be stones
before this farm then that struck
their chunks of undercoat loam.

Turquoise, red, bronze, gunmetal
flashed their decades on the roads of
river from the glass brilliance settled
in display rooms to the rough

rock and scum of these deep galleries.
I drift a nymph through a half-open
window on a risky tippet a breeze
could break as easy as a stone

in time. And you're there, old ghost,
with your sallow cheeks and your jokes
and exaggerations, what I thought was lost
pulling, bumping the emergency brake

cocked in the on position
until once more you're peering out
the window, a recurrence, a fish in
time—a snap. It's almost night.

28

SUNFISH

...Pound was an axe,
Chen was an axe, I am an axe
And my son a handle, soon
To be a shaping again, model
And tool, craft of culture,
How we go on.

—Gary Snyder, *Axe Handles*

LONG LAKE, MINNESOTA

When I was four, Father rowed
me out to weed beds of sunfish
so big our bobbers dove
red and white to deep green. Foolish

bundle I was, I romped and screamed
'till he tied me to the seat,
afraid I'd drown us both. I dream
those days now, bright

bobbers moving through sleep,
pulled down by life I can't control,
but then I was life that deep,
and Mother stood above the roll

of perfect waves, waving in a green
coat beside my brother, stung red
by hornets. On water I've never seen,
I try to get back to Brother Ted,

to Mother, but Father is gone
and the boat drifts in and out
of fog and dreams slipping down the dawn
of a thousand lakes, scattered about

like lost coins in the woods
of Minnesota. Now, years later
I look down from a jet, tied
to my seat, and blur the sun to water.

GAR

At night the boat noise seemed sharper in
Lake Tenkiller where the oarlocks
knocked as loud at each stroke as our light shone
deep into the water. Sunfish hung over rocks

among the branches of submerged oaks like Christmas
ornaments. Flathead catfish proved spontaneous
generation: mud to quick life at a near miss
of our arrows. But the gar never fooled us

and never tried. It was itself at night, snapping
the surface for cruising minnows, looking like
nothing else above or below, stopping
under fallen cattail brakes to strike

a pose that never worked. In the boat I picked one up,
my hands on both ends of the arrow, and stared
it in the face; it was only a foot long, but
it shook its stiff snake body and bared

its teeth until I thought the shaft would break
and it would swim the thin air to my eyes.
For it had always been my dragon: late
at night, stories from *Field and Stream* would rise

and solidify in pictures of a giant gar, stretched
across three sawhorses, bullet holes in its hide,
the fisherman, covered with blood, one hand on his catch
the other holding a pistol by his side.

Long ago on the Salt Fork, when the water was high,
Father and I walked a trestle out over the roar
and got dizzy looking through the ties
at water that seemed to carry the world. And there

in the swiftest current, was that snap, those teeth;
then that trestle seemed to fly.
Father towered above me, while from beneath
it rose, and I lay clinging to the ties.

OLD GHOST

When the weather doors swung shut
and the silver lies the mockingbird
told in the locust came true,
where were you, old ghost, so fast
and sad on those wings you called
work that were only small darknesses
pressing you farther into your bed
at night? Do those friends and family
who carry you and your flowers now
hear where the wind has stopped for you?

When the tornados came and ringed these hills
and oaks into your horror of nights
in the cellar, wife and children
talking low as the slap of rain on the tin door,
where were you, old ghost, so deep and lost
in your own dark circle that the clouds revolving
out of the night sky could only make it worse?
Does the flag they take from your last cold cellar
and fold make the hills ring brighter
this far from the lost sun?
Won't the wind still whip circles of dust
and rain into the springs and summers of our fall?

When the cancer drew you so tight on your bones
that we thought you an actor the nurses turned
there with the late light stiffening into your sheets,
where were you, old ghost, turning so fast
and sad on your laugh
that we might know no actor could play
your dark comedy so far into the fluorescent night?
Do these cars streaming for iron gates
leave you laughing to yourself
after your last bad joke,
or isn't that you, still suspended over the hole
when we leave, the rain drawn tight on our windshields?

SUNFISH

In this dream, years ago I am sick.
Mother is mopping my bedroom floor.
The pools she leaves are tablets of
sun where summer blows the curtains in,
teasing my fever out to the cool
morning and willows whipping near
a window. These pools are full
of small sunfish: longear, redear,
bluegill, pumpkinseed, green, warmouth.

Nothing is unusual about this.
Where her mop moves, the most
brilliant colors fresh water
can sustain find depth, dimension,
a place to live. The gray
tiles of the floor are neither defied
nor defiled, but truly cleansed, too deep
in dream to be dried by the willow-
breeze, too real by the trail of the mop
bucket to be stirred. This fever lifts

me up. I fashion a line of threads
from my sick-bed, a hook of a golden safety
pin. The pool where I fish has only
the depth of my love, of my dream;
orange and turquoise flesh darts and
flashes in a disc of light above which
Mother leans on her mop handle and laughs
and cries at what she has made,
at what I have stolen.

GRANDFATHER'S SESTINA

Your Browning 16 gauge, oiled and blued so smooth
that it looks automatic even before firing,
is still with me in the corner of a backroom closet,
slowly silting over, lost in my will
to fish, not hunt. This evening, through a window
blackbirds burst like flack from bare trees

and leave a black lattice, like the trees
lining the Salt Fork years ago, when the smooth
currents hissed on sand banks and windowed
a distant world beneath the brittle fire
of fall's late reflection. The sun soon will
take all of this down. We'll wear the black clothes

our dreams and tradition force us into. The closet
will become a way of speaking, and those trees
that sift the past from red to pink will
only return like this: a river smooth
as catfish skin, and the clear pop of firing
in the distance. Black fills the window

now. Sweating on my sheets, I hear the wind
all night and think of my first hunt. Close
under tamarack and limp vines, I fired
and saw a flurry near the base of a tree.
The rabbit still spins shrieking but smooth
in its circle of blood. When I try to will

this away, I can only hear your voice. "It will
die. Don't waste another shell." The wind
outside dies, and the dream is real, smoothed
into the weather. Through darkness toward the closet,
I feel my way from bed. Outside the trees
move against the house. Fire

pops on in the furnace. Again the dream of firing
returns as real as sharp branches, and I will
see this over and over: the brittle trees,
the trivial path of a rabbit in its unwinding
spool of blood, then your eyes, closed
by cancer, then Father's. The barrel is smooth

and cold from the closet though the room is warm. The fire
clicks off in the furnace below. The sun will
be up again soon. I watch the tops of the trees.

BAIT FOR THE TRAPS

You hit a jackrabbit in the road
and stop. It pinwheels through the dust
so you grab the hind feet and hit its head
against the bumper. Just

a few minutes before, you thumped
a watermelon at a roadside stand.
It was huge with fuzzy lumps
on its rind, maybe forty pounds.

You said it was full of pith and bought
a small, smooth one for a quarter from
the dirty little girl. When she caught
the coin, it shined like some

wild eye under a headlight from her hand.
Looking at the small melon on the seat
between us, I sulked. Now, as you stand
jerking fur from flesh, saying "bait

for the fish traps," I figure you must
have been right and fetch a gunny sack
from the back seat. I trust
you standing in the smell of the entrails, relaxed.

We drive to Ralph and Leo's place on the river.
Ralph limps out, half-paralyzed since youth.
Playing, he slipped from the porch and a sliver
of glass went into his spine. Leo's there too,

standing on the same porch waving.
"Bait," you laugh, swinging the sack in a leathery
hand, "and a melon," I squeak, hardly able
to carry it. We avoid the house; the brothers

don't ask many in since their mother died.
As long as a coffin, the fish trap drips
water and weed through its sides.
We hold the rope, and the brothers, hip

deep in mud, reach through a funnel of screen
and wire the slick corpse down. It turns
pink then gray as it drops between
them and washes in under some ferns.

Now, Ralph and Leo glisten on the bank,
their dark heads, arms and necks vivid; their
white, almost blue torsos. The pink
of the melon shows through where

Ralph cracks it on his knee then
is red when he digs the heart out.
We spit seeds, choke and talk on
sweetness. Sun turns the water white

as you snooze and they stare at small
clouds. I get up and solve the mystery
of their popcorn patch: each kernel
packed in a row. Now I see

a tight green sheath around everything,
but you're checking the trap so I run back.
At first, nothing, then dark catfish moving,
then one flips: white almost blue against black.

WEDDING

(August, 1973)

I with my new job
and you with your son, Chris,
decide that matrimony
is a must, so we kiss
sin and the 60's goodbye and head
for Elko, Nevada and a no questions,
no blood test, quick-fix solution.
The casinos, whore-house trailers,
Basque food joints and shopping malls
all say THIS IS THE PLACE
TO MAKE SACRED OUR LOVE,
and after we find the grand court house
the Justice of the Peace does,
as blue-haired court clerks
weep and clasp their hands
and Chris stares dumb
at his mom and new dad.
With no wedding rings,
we use those from your ears
then follow the Justice
to a private room where
he tells us some jokes
and of duck hunting in Cuba
before it fell—when everyone drove
Continentals and 300 ducks
could be shot in one day.
We say how much do we owe.
He says whatever it's worth.
So from a fat roll of twenties
you pull out a five and we go.

39

BIRTHDAY

September 1974

(Natchitoches, Louisiana)

for Judy

When St. Denis found this place,
the Red River ran through it.
Back 260 years, he probably waited
for the cool weather too.
Between us, the steam boats
up through the middle of town
stopped with slavery and a flood
that sent the river somewhere else,
leaving this ox bow, the Cane,
where I park by a boat ramp
and watch a black woman
lift a gleaming string of sunfish
and an old boy gun
his bass rig onto a trailer.

Since Max was born this morning,
the wind's been different all day:
more sluggish, thick with
the fried chicken smell of cotton seed oil
from a mill on the outskirts.
When the contractions started,
we drove the morning fast
through this wonder-soup,
even thicker with the cabbage smell
blowing in from distant paper mills.
It all stopped at the hospital
where the doctor took me aside,
showed me the x-ray of your pelvis
and said it would be a breech.
For what seemed hours
they had you somewhere else,
and I watched them wheel
a huge black woman
in and out of her own screaming.
The doctor went out for a sandwich
while we practiced our Lamaze charade.

In your first few puffs,
a foot came out and water
sprayed the labor room
to send the nurses screaming,
wheeling you away,
pushing me out to the quiet hall.

I tried to read, but
a whistle like a distant train
brought me back. It was you
in the delivery room, a scream
so high yet so abrupt, a quick
birth and no doctor. The nurse
with the *It's a Boy* button
seemed as unreal as Max later,
through the glass: purple,
bull-dog faced, head scarred.

A soft hand on my shoulder
turned me to a small black man
in sweat-stained work clothes.
"My wife, suh, she need a ride.
We got no car. They try to
make her ride the ambulance,
but that cost money we ain't got."
Down the hall was the huge woman
in a wheelchair with the hot baby
and a scowling white nurse.
The man took the baby, and I tried
not to stumble carrying the woman
to the car. His mother followed,
staring at me as if I were
from another planet.
In the rearview I saw the nurse
and heard crows and a distant voice:
"If anything happens, they'll sue."
But I thought of you, lying drained,
trying to make sense of the nurse's story.
We stopped for a rare traffic jam
on a bridge over the Cane.
Finally, at the other side,
we saw a half-mile stretch
of shiny cars, all with
headlights burning strong into the sun.

The black people inside were
as somber as their clothes
and flowers were bright.
After the funeral passed,
we started moving,
and the new breeze
through our windows blew
something more than hope
or loss. I carried my heavy load
into the house of wood and tar paper,
and the husband carried his light one.

Now that you and Max are sleeping,
I'm not ready to go home,
but have pulled over here
off of Main Street by this boat ramp
on the Cane to watch this fisherman
come in and this woman's
silver chain of sunfish.

AMERICAN FALLS

This brings us to us, and our set lines
set deep on the bottom. We're going all out
for the big ones. A new technology
keeps the water level steady year round.
The Company dam is self cleaning.
In this dreamy summer air you and I
dreamily plan a statue commemorating
the unknown fisherman.

—Richard Hugo, *Making Certain It Goes On*

THE MISSOURI

On your first dam at Toston
a farmer took his life
in spite of his lush fields
where you backed up green
then spun down on the heads
of spawning rainbows.
We still see them,
shaking in mist above the
torrent, swimming nowhere
to a home in their heads.
The farther we move
down the divide you drain
the clearer our mistakes
become in your opacity.
Your rims and breaks
dwarf our own erosions.
Coming out of your late youth,
flashing gold-eye in your
sluggish green, you slow down
at Fort Peck to swell
what's behind in losses
the size of giant northerns.
Below that dam, paddlefish
flop out their prehistoric comedy
sucking silt through their gills
for a living. You know that
joke too, rolling your shoulders
one last time, then moving on
to the hard work of the flatlands.

OFF THE ROAD:

for *Charles Kuralt*

(in West Yellowstone)

I fished fat Muddlers of chukar
feathers on holes two and three
of the Madison then went to town
for a snack and saw you
wandering aimless, benevolent
between signs for souvenirs,
flies, maps and tackle. "On the Road?"
I asked. "No, off the road," you said.
Back in water, I heard your voice,
your causes, concerned as the looks
on baffled bears staring out
of barrel traps. I saw small
risings near seams in current
and thought of reservoirs
we keep building, beautiful
stillnesses before them, streams
dying behind them, our lives
losing direction and our dreams
becoming at once more frightening,
complex and forgettable.
But your voice is still there:
water behind migrating cranes
in Nebraska, sunrise hiss and lap
of ice-lined shores on the Great Lakes,
or rivers burning up in fog through
oaks in Ozark valleys—as if there's
no trap here; things aren't really
that bad. The dams will
wear away without breaking.

BEFORE THE LAST CLEAN RAIN

(Cortland, New York)

From the Tioughnioga or Factory Brook, Father
came home. And I, just six, ran
to the kitchen through hazelnut
thickets out back to see his catch:
on newspaper and checked oilcloth,
a whitefish and two smallmouth still
breathing. Cortland spring made New York
a gray, wet beginning, spotted by sun
on the Finger Lakes in bright planks
to deep boulders. The red eyes of rock
bass were more than early stars against
this gray when he stayed late hurling
spoons the size of sparrows against
the night wind and caught a lake trout,
its meat the color of sunrise.
My brother and I went to the waterworks
and saw trout like huge absences.
Otter creek behind our house held
eternity until it went dry and left
brook trout like Mother's silver hairpin
in wet pockets behind rocks.
Later we waded the creeks and marshes
near Virgil. I wore a gaudy watch
with metallic greens and blues marking
white under red hands. I reached
down that day to catch a bright striped
dace, and it went under stopping there
somewhere in the late afternoon
in one of those bars of sun
driven before the last clean rain.

A FIELD OF FLOWERS

Williams is long
dead now. My father
just died young.

But today I found
a dried petal in
Williams' *The Broken Span*

among my father's
books, remembering
when I was nine

how, while we
moved from New York
to Oklahoma,

the tarp blew
from the trailer
and Father's books

and papers scattered
across the highway and
into a field of flowers.

AT A GRAIN ELEVATOR
IN SALT FORK, OKLAHOMA

"Dod gam prices," said the farmer
in his overalls stained red with
riverbottom soil and black with grease.

I didn't know if he restrained himself
because of me or because of God,
for I was a pink young boy in shorts,

an English professor's son among farmers
and next to me, Grandfather, a farmer himself
trying to cover up my voice with his.

I, too, thought the prices unfair,
but, for no apparent reason, Grandfather said,
"My grandson here's a real hard worker."

All turned from prices to a clean boy
as the trucks roared on to the scales out front.
"Dod gam if he isn't," said the silence inside.

On the way home in the old gunmetal chevy
with yellow grasshoppers the size of clothespins
sputting from windshield to pigweed ditches,

I said,"I'm no worker, Grandad."
In the rearview dust rose for a mile.
"I know," he said. "I know."

SALT FORK

Come clear from the salt flats
then stain yourself red through
the bottoms where gourds shine
and turtles point their heads
lightward. Swell your seams
where gar snaps at redhorse.
Wear down the creosote in pillars
of rattle-planked bridges to
Lamont, to Hunter, to Pond Creek,
to towns hemmed by sun blurred
through chinaberry and sandplum
thicket. Wear redbud reflections
when your water is high; wear
the thistles and pods of a new
life when you go down for late fall.
Take with you the horse, shot
in the white diamond of its forehead
and left in your tamaracks. Take
the bones of the farmers who leaned
on their shotguns. Soak to mud
the beams of barns and houses, spun
up in tornados and dropped
where channel cat flashed in wheat
fields while the night storm passed.
Take them all until your color
is a deep red dream in the Gulf.

LAMONT, OKLAHOMA

Opening a door for the first time,
I walk into a hall with windows
and planks of sun.
It is probably too late.
This wind that I have kept
calling upon hasn't matched my steps
in any way. Always, a few steps
before me is what the water becomes
below the surface. And holding
his breath for the last time,
my father might still be a child
in that town with a silver water tower
and a park below it. He could
be walking under those locust trees
in a world that he had finally
decided to call play and get lost
like cicadas buzzing in secret
behind limbs. Like them
he might have spent my life
burrowing in roots while
playmates of his first twelve years
spun tops at marbles above him.
A wind of red dust would still
have capped any evening sun
in its usual charged deception.
And the tiger moths that whirred
and sucked the orange mouths
of the lilies after dark
might have been his lessons
where he taught me how to die on
a street where death was as real as the
way branches meet at the top of an arc.

A FAMILIAR PLACE

(Stillwater, Oklahoma)

As we hunted frogs with BB guns,
my friend and I knew our place,
walking lightly behind tall ferns
before dark water like isinglass.

We had followed the bellow of a bullfrog
to its head, bigger than a lily pod,
beside a slanted, rotting snag.
But when we aimed, behind that wood

something moved. We craned our necks
and saw her face first under his,
then, against his hips her bobby socks
and next to her his boots, her shoes,

her shorts, his jeans all wadded up.
They moved and moved then motion locked;
she screamed then tensed her hips.
When I saw her tears, I slowly backed

up the bank, knocking loose a stone
that clattered down and splashed so loud
the frog ducked under, and the man,
uncoupled, slick and pink, stood

up and grabbed a real gun: blacker,
heavier than either of ours;
so we skidded and stumbled up the shore
while through budding trees, the early stars

sputtered too bright too soon
like the last look of hate on her face
as cold, white and still as the moon
yet as familiar as that place.

MAIL-ORDER SESTINA

(Ulysses, Kansas)

It figures that your mother was a mail-order
bride: Brooklyn Girl Marries Kansas Farmer—
that you and your new father didn't speak
for six years. "Tell her to pass
the mashed potatoes"—that the farm dusted over
bad and you sat in it for summers before it grew

back. But you accepted it, grew
used to the older step brothers and sister ordering
you around until you ran off and got over
it in the only tree for miles, watching some farmer
turn the late stubble to dust. It wouldn't pass.
This father wouldn't speak.

But one day he got the horse to speak,
dragging it to death behind the truck. You grew
as other animals died. Your rabbit, Pinky, passed
like this: the cat bit off its head. Order
restored that night, the stiff-jawed farmer
said,"Pass the rabbit," as the skies slid over

prop drones then webs of vapor trails, over
the dust that never settled, the catbird that spoke
all night. For years the short, burned sons of farmers
around you married daughters who knew their language, grew
their children young. For you the orders
stopped. You stuck by your mother as she passed

her arms through rooting pigs until the pain passed
from work that never fit. Years later, over
Kansas backroads, you returned and found order
in the rafters of your attic, chickens speaking
through carcasses of rabbits. This grew.
Once you returned to a chinchilla farm,

fur balls scratching sand around your bed. Forms
darker than rusting sheds followed summers, passing
beyond where you drove the tractor, monotony grooving
the sun away in wind that didn't quit in over-
cast or gullies scorched to cracking. Speaking
his first words to you, that Father ordered

more than you could take. So you left the farm,
hopped in a pink '57 Chevy and passed
from him and the world until you grew.

AMERICAN FALLS

At 4:00 a.m., I drove to American Falls
through twenty miles of southern Idaho
to where the Snake stopped between canyon walls
behind the dam then roared out below.

Over the foaming forebay on catwalks
old men had already established themselves,
eyes fixed on current-bent rods, backs
bent to the spray. And from the swells

they pulled flopping rainbows, huge balloons
of flesh. They used night crawlers, sucker-meat on
cheap hooks with lots of weight. I fished spoons
that only worked for a thin hour of dawn.

Between cement walls and the turbines, the fish
were ours or chopped up before the river
was itself again. And the old men, fresh
for death, knew this better than I, whether

or not they showed me their stringers.
No one had to mention humility under the
terrible sound of water getting thinner
with one place to go. When we'd see

Union Pacific scream over the top of the dam,
it was only a whisper to us, like the lines
in our fingers, whistling a secret hymn
deep into the howl, searching for signs

of present-tense rainbows. The smoke
of a phosphate plant rose with dead fish
above the banks, always out to tell us no
and keep us trying, flicking our wrists

toward flux. Now it's all framed. They're dead.
Their clusters of fat trout swam out of time.
A smooth new dam is there instead—
no forebay, just water in a hard, thin line.

BEHIND THE WATER

The water found us out,
silvering our wrists,
waving weeds clear under
our reflections,
freezing to lids on our bays,
lakes, and even our rivers.
We prayed with it,
we drowned ourselves in it,
we stood by it
making our tongues go funny
in our mouths to sound like it.
But the water wasn't interested.
It was carrying the smell of
mountains deep to salmon waiting
on the continental shelf.
In its current it had
every direction. In its color
it carried its past. In dark
beds on cold mornings,
we lay under covers
and heard it on our roofs,
spelling its other name in our sleep.
Awakening in mountain tents,
we learned how to sing
without opening our mouths.

WIND ON THE MADISON

(Norris, Montana)

The swells and hummocks
that splay this water out
in sheets make wading here
a mystery. Against me, the current.
Above me, a redwing rides still.
The wind drives me out of myself.
When it all dies, the caddis hatch
comes, wings burning the late sun
into my eyes. I have been here
before, digging for pills or flies,
waiting for spring to get it
over with and bring the water down
clear below Ennis.

And the wind will be back,
reeling through cliffs,
not knowing where it's from.
Then I might wade the gravel tongue
from an island of alder and find
that I and the currents have changed.
But tonight I will spin the river
back and stand by my house
to feel the new weather.

THREE RIVERS IN ONE

Where the land divides,
the earth cools, grows smaller
and shrugs, throwing up three ranges
that even now buckle higher
as the moon whirls full to fingernail,
these rivers come and stay
to show you where you stand.

The Gallatin splits high pines
and sheer rock faces, tacked
to the overthrust,
then rolls narrow and deep
on boulders to show you
how fast you can forget
all the faces of the riffles
but never the one face
of the pools.

The Madison rides round rocks down
to sand hummocks and weed,
always into the wind:
air and water waging their
brilliant wars against the earth.
Stand in the current.
Forget your name.

The Jefferson knows the indirection
of low hills, riding deep
over meadow-loam to each bend and undercut,
swirling silt from the holes
to throw a haze over the
straightest rock runs.
When those closest to you fall away,
rejoice in the way this knotted country
forgets itself so quickly.

Three names, vague hints
at the sound of water:
three syllables each,
rolling from your tongue
when you see what will be here
after words return to wind,
making small v's on the slack Missouri.

PSALMS, ODES
AND RANTS

I looked for hamburger references in the Bible.
I was certain that there must be an overlooked reference
to a burger in the Book of Revelations. Maybe the
Four Horsemen of the Apocalypse like hamburgers.

—Richard Brautigan, *So the Wind Won't Blow It All Away*

DUCT TAPE PSALM

Take our broken lives
in thy bright grasp,
and make them to hold
fast until the bad weather.
Make our down jackets
to look like nuclear waste dumps.
Hold plastic table cloths
to the torn roofs of our
convertibles and seal
our cardboard windows.
Make our hoses and pipes to
spray sideways in many directions.
Hold our wrists tight
for the criminal while he
does his grim work.
Encircle our boots to
let water in and keep it there.
Mend our styrofoam coolers
when we glut them to cracking
with fish. Bond with Rubbermaid
to keep our trash
from the raging dogs,
and lash our dirtbikes
tight to the butts of our Winnebagos.
Hold slabs of contraband
to our bodies when we cross
national borders.
Make our Bibles, manuals and almanacs
to look like metalloid blocks
from Uranus. Never let us down.
Come loose when we least expect it.

ODE TO ROUGH FISH

I speak for the carp, fat on mud-bloat
and algae, orange-lipped lipper of algae surfaces,
round rotter of the banks of hydroelectric rivers.
Not the quick thin-meated trout
darting his pretty life in the rare rocks of high streams.

Ah, and the rooting sucker, round tubed mouth distended
to bobble rocks, worms, offal, whatever
he can turn up without himself turning up.

Yes, here's to you, scumsuckers of the stagnant
reservoirs and sludge-filled rivers, livers on
waste discharge, suckers down of anything we can
slop on you at our worst moments.

Long live you who will live long whether
we say so or not, who would as soon wallow in
the hollow of a bloated river-soaked moose corpse
as live up to a size 20 Coachman on a 7X tippet.
You live up to nothing and we will never live you down,
for you horrid-mouthed mouthers of death and
worse than death have found something stronger
than the slats of your hard flat scales.

Where a trout jumps for the thin wings of a fresh-
hatched caddis, you jump for nothing but air
through the filth and oil slicks.
Where a trout darts at a nymph behind a rock, you
could care less; you move the sonofabitching rock
and all the mud around it. Yes, you too will
find the nymph and eat it, but you will also eat
the mud and love it.
Yes, you love mud.
Mud is your guts; thus, your guts are always distended
in thick slabs of carp meat—sucker meat.
You and your wallowing, blubbery truth.
You and your truth that has made a heaven of sewage.

Why didn't they call *you* rainbow or golden,
for if God gave a promise and warning
in one fell swoop,
you are it,
arching from your black lake
completely clear and shining of water
then falling back
splat.

MORE CARP

for Brad Donovan

The lake, windless down its miles
of canyon, is pocked in polka dots
of spawning carp. They flop out
potboilers of cheap romance, streaking
gold below the boat toward brief
rendezvous with a sky they must find
intriguing or why would they clap
in unison, a dozen schools or so?

Some hang down six feet below,
fins hunched up like trenchcoat
collars, 'till the shot rings out;
where, we can only guess.
They know. Fat shoulders flexed, they
shoot to live, those chubby bullets
bent on air, then falling back into
themselves. Proteus would be proud

then something else real quick,
in and out of water chopped dumb
then back to plain reflection.
As if one wearing Evening in Paris
thought this oar a lamp post, six
more bash the flattened paddle after
her, and she vees then clears the
surface over the wallow of hot

pursuit. Now they all file into
the Bolshoi; their prima she's
eight pounds or more and draws the
rest to stag leaps, entrechats
and worse until the wind comes up
and puts this down, this stupid plan
that doesn't work, that leaves us bobbing
silly in our boat, that makes more carp.

FOR THE ARMADILLOS

We've noticed how
you've come up as far as Kansas
curled in maimed half-moons by the road.
What do you do that for?
Won't the bobcat still peel you
slick as abalone?
Won't you still surprise us
like a walking rock
or shock us as you bolt from ditches,
running like we never knew you could?
Go ahead and butt your snout into
those bugs for now.
Go ahead and make your little
feet rattle through burrs and thistles
while your body floats like
the moon above them.
But what did you come here for?
To have some farm girl fling
you wounded from a bridge
on the Cimarron,
thinking that she is doing
you a favor,
thinking that you
are some kind of half-assed
nightmare turtle?
Some folks say you taste like rabbit.
Others say you carry leprosy,
but most of us just glimpse
a bubble and ears poking up
from the asphalt
and drive on.

A BLUE SHIRT

Half of my back yard has snow on it:
deep. Half of it doesn't. In the
garage, I'm smoking fish and incidentally
whatever else is in the garage.
I like the smell of the cherrywood
burning so I keep walking outside
then back in to "check the fish."

I'm wearing bluejeans, a blue L.L. Bean
shirt and a lined leather vest
and don't even feel phoney about it.
All of them are starting to smell like
smoke. Now I'm out in the yard and
I hear the sound of someone clearing
his throat and spitting. I can't see him

until I look up at the balcony of
an old white house several houses from mine.
He's out in the sun; he's wearing a
blue shirt. He's seen me. I poke a cherry
twig at a patch of mud, clearing it from grass
near the snow bank. The smell of cherrywood
is all over the neighborhood. I hate him.

MAGPIE

In tall firs
my eye is as sharp as
its blackness shining.
Some day I might shit
on you as you walk to
work. Forgive me now.
Crush my brothers and
sisters to food on asphalt
and I will eat. No qualms,
no frightened flapping
like ravens. Forgive me my
blue-green metallic presence.
Be fooled by my white spots.
Let me gawk and stumble
through your suburbs,
sometimes mistaken for
the cats that try to kill me.
I am your West.
I am the small flying cow
of your doubt. Why be
subtle? Don't the wide
blue horizons do something
to you too?
So walk under this tree
thinking. I'll start a
franchise. I'll call in
my friends.

SESTINA ON THE BRITISH COARSE

What we call sucker, chub and carp are coarse
to them. I have dreamed of lords with fly
rods and tweeds beside the chalk-bottomed Test.
Granted, that's no myth. Yeats' Irishman,
the freckled one "who goes to a grey place
on a hill/In grey Connemara clothes/At dawn

to cast his flies" still works his way down
galleries of watercolor. And, of course,
the stone is still "dark under froth" in that place
at "the down-turn of his wrist/When the flies
drop in the stream." The dream is real. The man
does exist. But you'd think that he'd detest

the barbel, tench, chub and carp—detest
the coarse. He doesn't. As I walked down
to Trafalgar Square, a picture of a man
on a magazine drew me to the rack. The coarse
tweed of his jacket was dotted with real flies
and covered with slime. He'd won first place

with the twenty-pound carp, out of place
in his arms, held as a chubby child for the contest
judges, held as if it might fly,
so fat and zeppelin-like it was. Then it dawned
on me, British or not, his face—his coarse
smile was almost American! That man's

smile rode his carp like the first Englishmen
rode the Mayflower. I paid the clerk, found a place
to sit by a Wimpy's, and opened my *Coarse
Fishing Mail*. Within were lists of contest
winners beside the hoops of live-holding nets, down
by other ads for dough-bait, chum catapults and fly-

sized hooks. I paused and watched the pigeons fly
up and light on Admiral Nelson then read about a man
with a fat carp under each arm, caught fresh just down
the Thames; a boy with eight bulging tench, placed
on the bank grass of Regents Park Lake, testing
the light like a necklace of huge opals. On the coarse

have mercy, Yeats. These people and fat fish don't fly
in the face of great Art and the wise. These fishermen
know carp too can be "as cold/And passionate as the dawn."

ODE TO THE OTHER

When I steal a weekday
from work and drive pavement
to gravel to dirt so the river
might be mine alone,
you're there
from miles of water
splashing upstream toward me,
lunging to beat me
to the foot of the riffle.
If I'm fishing bait, you'll have flies
and eye me coldly under your
L.L. Bean hat. If I'm fishing flies,
you'll sling your sculpin to the foot
of my steamer's swing.
If I'm sick of the world,
you'll ask me how I'm doing
and show me your fat creel.
If they're not biting,
you'll follow my retreat upstream,
telling me that I should
have been here yesterday.
If I've caught a three pounder,
you'll tell me about the four pounder
you just released.
If you come too close,
something will go wrong with my reel,
and I will scream obscenities at it
until you go away.
I've always tried to avoid you,
hiding in alder thickets,
hiking miles to the heart
of wilderness meadows, but
it's no good. You're always there,
clashing with my mood,
darting for my holes,
catching me glancing sideways
while you catch my fish,
sullenly watching me gloat
as I catch yours.

I suppose you're as close
as I'll ever come to death
before death: that long river
leading deep into willow thickets,
hours into darkness,
and you, sloshing up out of brambles,
your waders sucking mud like the sound
of mating pigs to ask, "Having any luck?
What you using? Should have been here yesterday."

NYMPHING THE SNOW BALL OF THE UPPER MADISON

Before the dam at Ennis
slows and warms it,
this water is so clear
I wade into inches already feet
and fight hard just to stay in place.

Casting Hare's Ears upstream
and stripping line down
to keep a tight feel
for the bump, I might
as well be waltzing with
Amazons on Jupiter.

My line isn't right and
sinks fast and against me
with shifting winds. I
strike at anything but life.

Upstream, the only other
man for miles has a wand
that taps the river to
a tight fugue
of floating line.

He's a clock that ticks
stone fly nymphs
down the trickiest riffle
on pebbles to the dropoff.

He looks up at me, whalloping
away to beat the wind.
I could easily be a tree.
I'd swear he studies the lay
of the water I've stopped.

FOR THE CRAWLERS

We've watered the lawn for you again.
And even in the sun you're wallowing
up and rooting the grass for rot.
It's your luck the robins don't
like us or the yard would turn
Italian dinner. We've seen
you sliding over the cool, wet
evenings of America,
crazed children with flashlights
homing in. Some day their youth,
touched, will shoot back like you do.
Our shrinks choose snakes, the fools.
They are insomniacs but never take
the time to go out and look down
into the grass at midnight.
Sometimes you appear as fishnets,
bellied out over our gardens
toward the moon. And after rain
your deaths are as worthless as
broken shoelaces on our sidewalks.
To bring you up, we've played the earth
like a fiddle on boards and buried
electrodes in our back yards.
We've dozened you up in styrofoam cups.
We've even made quiche out of you.
You poor sonofabitches.
For you, crucifixion would be peanuts.
We've pinched you apart,
slipped your gobs on hooks
and spit on you for good luck.

THE CHIGGER MARTYRS

Stories say you're alive
inside your bite,
under our night scratching.
So, when fresh from summer grasses,
we awaken and traipse
to our bathroom lights
to see where you pock
our ankles and crotches,
is our panic any wonder?
Is it perverse
that we would scratch your lumps
to bleeding then douse
the wounds with after-shave,
nail polish, whatever
the bathroom shelves would offer?
We imagine our itching your comfort—
our pain your pain.
puffing and hooting
back to our beds,
we figure it's been worth it,
our bodies like Russia
burned around the Nazis.
And in the morning
we view the carnage
like true patriots,
scorning those traitors
who would say,
"It was all a farce:
chiggers eat and run."
So we return staunch
to the summer grasses,
wearing your bites
like little badges
in our underwear.

FOR ABRAHAM AND IZAAK WALTON

And lo he took his sons unto the brook
and bade them fish quietly and patiently.
And when their lines many times
had encircled the ends of their poles
and their reels had made many tangles,
he wept before them saying, "That son
who unto me would bring peace, he shall
I call unto the station wagon
and give candy and pop."
And lo a wond'rous silence fell
upon them, for they knew not why
their father would spread his bounty
before them for not fishing.
And then it was that many heavy fish
came unto his bait and many sounds came
unto him from the station wagon.
And the sounds of empty candy
wrappers begat many pitches both high
and low of grumbling.
And the grumbling begat lamentations of
the late hour, and the late hour begat a
longing for that which they had come to call TV.
And lo he walked unto the car and
spake unto them saying many words
of which he had not thought himself capable.
And in his anger, he threw his rod
unto the back and made the door
to slam upon it.

IS THE OUZEL STUPID?

Though you've spent
your life practicing,
you still don't seem
to understand
how water works.
You aren't supposed
to bounce
that clear pool
then hop the gravel
bottom of the
fastest current
like a robin on
a courthouse lawn—
or flit back
to your rock
and dip like a fat
boxer at a shadow
without arms.
Birds don't work
that way.
Jesus, nothing works
that way.
I'd sooner believe
a small gray
meatloaf
had paddled
the Mississippi to
the Continental Divide.
Bring me my Polaroids.
Bring me
my binoculars.
Bring me
the God damned
bird book.

BIRD BOOK BLUES

What can I say?
I like the blue ones
with orange flashes
or the orange ones
with black flashes.
See, there's one in
that little tree with
the broad, sort of
greenish-yellow leaves—
right next to that big
plant with the long
slanting stems and
the tiny blue flowers.
That one's song sounds
like a phone left
off the hook for
over a minute, and
that one is eating
the seeds out of
those long brown things
that grow in swamps.
And I like the little
bitty ones, the ones
with black caps that
don't make much noise.
But do they make the
winters worth while—
at least until those
fat brown ones come
and turn purple or blue
when the sun hits them
right. You know—
the ones that will peck
cat crap if given
half a chance and huddle
in clumps on the driveway
even after you start

the car. But then spring
comes and there are lots
of those big gray ones
that look like their
breasts have rusted
for all the rain.
They move in such a way
that you might actually
say they bob—or at least
until a late heavy snow.
Then they don't bob
so much. They just sort
of sit there on the green
spots between the snow like
they wish they were dead.

ODE TO MY WADERS

I'm in you once more my clown pants,
ready for the river, slick rocks or not.
Again, you'll buoy me up in deep rapids
and send me elbow first to the rock bottom.
And it will inevitably be
November with ice in the water,
and I will arrive home stiff and funny.
I will cross fences in you and you
will tear at the crotch. I will run from
bulls in you and you will trip.
When I am most confident, you will
slowly leak.
When I am strong, you will fill to
the knees and make me sit on the bank
and smoke.
When I am weak, you will lure me into
water past my waist and I will stay there.

Once I filled you up on the river
and took you off at the bottom of a pool.
I broke your suspenders and shot up
like a trout; later you washed to the
foot of the pool looking more grim
and detached than ever.

But I will patch you and cover you
with gobs of glue.
For you are my bottom half in
water and will always move in another world,
ballooning under me,
squeaking at the hinges like a small bird
when I walk.

Tomorrow to find leaks I will
hang you from a tree and fill
you with water. You won't look
like me at all.

DRIVING THE BLIZZARD

Breathe deep! No hurt, no pardon
out here in the cold with you
you with your back to the wall.

—Adrienne Rich, *Orion*

MAKING IT IN TIME

The road dips so much here
the car shakes and we
are driving where they
paved a buffalo wallow.
For years buffalo dented
the mountainsides,
the riverbanks,
the high plains—
hooves in the air
nosing wildflowers
and grinding the sweet grass
into a breeze more permanent
than this road where
you spill your coffee,
I hug the wheel,
and we wonder if
we will make it in time.

HAMBURGERS

for Richard Brautigan

Today we are eating
our hamburgers for
Richard. We don't
know what else to do.

...

Today we are holding
our hamburgers like
pools on the Gallatin
hold leaves.

...

Today, in the Eagles
Bar, Montana has made
winter out of October:
out there, wet snow.
In here, the fruit
fly on the edge
of the whiskey glass
we've set up for him
doesn't know where
else to go.

...

As tiny as it is,
we still have no
problem seeing that
its eyes are red.

···

Today our hamburgers
taste like Bozeman
Creek sounds, running
low beneath us, then
under Main Street,
the Bozeman Hotel,
the open sky.

···

Today, at his ranch,
the kitchen clock is still
full of bullet holes.

···

Today we do not
let our hamburgers slip.
We decided that they
should be double-burgers,
loaded. When we ordered
we said, "Give us
double-burgers, loaded."

···

And now, we are almost
finished. There are
two miracles:
1. Nothing has fallen
to our plates.
2. His glass is full.

MERCURY VAPOR

It contracted the distances
of night in Oklahoma,
constellating the plain
with bright pinpoints
to keep the lost intact
or the night-plowing farmer
home to the circle
of light in his brain.
Private north stars are
enough in warm air when
the wanderer knows his place,
loves illumination and fathoms
it's as real as the June bugs
and moths that bump themselves
silly then buzz down dazed.
I keep that in mind
driving Montana, ascending
this valley of the Missouri.
I stood all day in wind
at ten below, fishing
a frozen reservoir, and watched
a sky too cold to snow
sift crystals through a weak sun.
In the early night, my hands
flex just enough to start the car,
turn the wheel, make the motions
necessary to move me toward
what I know better.
But even on the open road,
heater howling, the miles
before me almost prove too much.
The half moon above and the rivers
of blown snow whispering
to drifts on the highway
hold me to the present 'till I pull
to the side by a bridge.
In stillness, all I hear
is the thunder of distance
frozen to scattered points of light,

their isolation so intense
they become inevitable tokens
of the lost: Grandfather and
Grandmother, close, hard and blue;
Father, a dim flickering
in the impossible distance;
my friend Richard, a harsh,
loony blinking behind trees
where no farm should be.
The roar of a semi pulls me
back to the road, and I drive
toward the violet wake of the sun,
so deep the red of receding
tail lights almost blends
in a blur of snow and tears,
and I follow as fast
as the ice will let me.

CANYON FERRY

(Townsend, Montana)

for Vern Troxel

I

November 24

A white line of rocks
puts an end to water
where gulls turn the distance
inside out.

I'm driving nowhere
in a parked car,
looking at a line
marked with white cloth.

Mallards spatter low
across the mouth
of this cove.
The water could be frozen a mile out,
but here the wind
has built all morning
and settled between
waves for the afternoon.

Not a bite for two hours
and the yellow grass whips
high over pockets of shade
on rocks where snow remains.

I hurried so hard to get here
I've forgotten the beer.
Dumb gulls stumble up shore
thinking I've left guts.
Smart ones stay high
in weather like this.

II
December 20

It's 15 below.
The ice is a foot thick,
smooth and clear of snow
where each catch flashes
yards out coming in to
inches and the dark circle,
boiling face up,
too real as the air
shocks water solid
to stiffen it there.

Up the banks, willow
and alder redden the cove
to the crystal thunder
of distance to pine foothills
to the bare white domes coming
in and out of clouds.

A blizzard up the valley
makes the straight ice
horizon whiter to nothing
then the warmer air
and the first flakes on me,
too soft for a far away
horror, but thick, leaving
me, my equipment, my car
nothing in the distance.

III
January 30

Ice slammed white down
the valley on a river turned
lake holds me up winter
on winter. Wait for the

solid foot near shore
and drive out on the plain,
station wagon secure.

Make holes in ice,
set poles,
drink coffee,
run for bite,
slip,
hit head,
crack like rifle shot.

Sky on ice is blue on white
but the world under me, what's that?
Gray to black from light under snow?
Something dying hard?

The wind comes up. I'm in my car
fishing out the window. Hand
holding pole is on my heart when
I feel the dim beat and jerk.
Wind from mountains in gray rivers
of pine whips down. Flick on heat
and radio then turn car around.

What are these
flopping on the seat next to me?
I'm dreaming sex but there's a light
not mine under ice.
Lee to open buzzing door
I'm cutting orange and crimson roe.
Between my beer and near concussion,
the radio plays a song called
The Corpses of Trout and Perch.
My hands can't feel.
Pure flesh leaves me huddled
by the heater breathing slow
under the walls of weather.

IV

March 15

Spring come early has
gotten the best of ice,
so I row the bands of water
near shore while the rest
of winter floats miles wide
between me and the far bank.
Now, across a slush plain,
gulls peck guts, skin
and spine thawed from
the little killings
of three months' ice fishing.
Luck's as dead as the winter,
so I shuck sweater and coat
for sun in the bottom of
my boat on water so still
it holds mountains down to
their farthest cedars
and looks more solid
than my vast ice island.
Sleep comes easy these
days, and I dream of
jumping rainbows that
never come down but keep
the sky to themselves until
they flash ruby sides
against the blue curve of
what used to be heaven.
I wake to a new wind
and thunder of ice blown
to shore crushing up in shard
mountains like the broken dome
of my dream until
even the heaviest clothes
aren't enough.

DRIVING THE BLIZZARD

Headlights don't go far in this.
Flakes blur to a thousand beams,
coming in hard but never hitting,
assuming the form of vision itself
until the highway whitens
and joins the rest of Wyoming.
There's nothing left
but to pull over and hope
for the plow.
Starting the car
occasionally for heat,
watching the dim lights
of close traffic joining me
on the shoulder, I still buzz
from twelve hours of driving.
I step out into the howl.
My U-Haul trailer has a flat.
I thought it was the constant
pull of the wind, ice, on-coming trucks,
and weight of my load.
I get Father's blanket
from the trunk. Back inside,
its likeness of a bear
covers me chin to boots.
The Oklahoma dust
in Grandmother's Chevy
is red on my finger
where I wipe it across the dash.
In this smothering whiteness,
their deaths are fresh on me:
the quick flights
between Montana and Oklahoma
for the impossible hospitals
then the funerals.
But the blanket is warm,
the car runs
and I was born near this dust;
so sleep comes and goes
as oblique as snow.

In the U-Haul, Father's books
and Grandmother's appliances
pause between lives,
protected from the deepening drifts.
No one belongs here—
just before the pass
above Cheyenne; so I pull
the blanket tighter around me
and follow the dust back home
to its smell through screen porches
where summer storms swung in
like purple curtains,
driving us to the root cellar.
There everything stopped
in a few drops
between cracks in the door.
We were a family,
safe from the dark funnels,
dangling their lazy grace
over wheatfields outside.
Then the hail came
'till its din trailed off to tapping.
It is a highway patrolman
at my window. The blizzard has stopped.
The revolving yellow light
of the plow sweeps the snow.
I leave the trailer in its drift
and follow a line of cars
down to Little America
where I join the sleeping crowds
on carpet-muffled floors.
In the dark, children whimper,
an old man next to me coughs
and from a card game
in a distant room,
a cowboy keeps yelling,
"Wahoo, Powder River."
I can't sleep and I can't wake up,
and the Powder River becomes snow
in my headlights,

and the tuning-fork hum
of Father's new watch
under Grandmother's pillow
becomes the howl again,
and the bear on top of me keeps turning
near the end of a long winter.

SOD FISHING:
A DREAM FOR THE END OF WINTER

I stop by a vacant lot in my
Oklahoma home town. It used
to be a pond where I ice fish
near my new home in Montana,
but now it's sodded over.
Ice holes are gopher holes,
and my childhood buddies are
catching fat rainbows on
cut rainbow roe.

I'm not ready for this,
only a fly rod in my car.
I use it anyway, borrowing
a gob of spawn, catching
a fat female and using her spawn
grown white and rotten in her.

The next hole I try has
a fish that fights hard
but flops up throught the sod.
It's a rough fish with wide scales
and a cat's mouth. I hit its
head and leave it to rot,
but dry, the scales are soft fur
and I'm ashamed.
I ease it through the sod and
watch it wobble half-stunned down.

In the next hole, the bite comes
fast and the fight is harder.
This time I pull the howling head
of a panther out. Next to me
my wife, who doesn't care much
for fishing, asks, "What's that?"
"A panther," I say and cut the line.

In the next hole the bite doesn't
come, so I walk toward the car
then turn to see the arc of my rod.
This time the pull is steady
like a snagged boot,
but when my line is nearly in,
blue popcorn spills up from the sod
then back. I balk at the loss
until what's forcing it comes:
a perfect rainbow crusted with popcorn.
I gloat. This one's not going back.
My buddies, now grown old
and cranky, clap.

NEAR MYTHS

They make a song for their dogs, up North,
four-letter words only, the kind
real dogs can use, bark-bark, woof-
woof, and so on—you know;
and every night they go to call
the big one—*Pavlov! Pavlov!*—
strictly home on obedient paths in the snow.

—William Stafford, Fictions

MOCKINGBIRD

Everything you do
is a part of me.
I will sing all night
if I have to.
I will hear you in
your dreams asking
why in hell. All
the next day I will tell you
sitting in my tree
above your house.
And in the willows by
the pond you will not
only see your reflection.
You will hear it.
If you are a sad young woman
you will recognize your own
song in the rushes:
your grandmother giving
birth to your father,
a child playing with a toy,
the wail of bomb sirens.
They are nothing new
to me. My wings are walls
aginst your sky. When
I fly, your voice is no more
to me than an eddy in
the wind, but even then
when I pass, you will
recognize it.

DUCKS

For one thing, they're
not as big as swans.
A duck probably wouldn't
have made much of an
impression on Leda.
She might even have
laughed. But on their
high, cold flights,
their pain must be
considerable. On TV
a fat duck used to
bring money down for
Groucho. That one
and the one that
fluttered toward my gun
on a Louisiana lake
seemed as sad
as they were fat.
On late Novembers,
dozens of wiggling
Groucho brows have found
their way out of dreams,
moving a sad silly song
in and out of the wind,
across a brittle sky.

WONDER BAIT

It sounds like sex.
When the boys lashed
Ulysses to the mast
and the sirens started,
this bait was
in the stars.
Lower it in a Ball jar
down through an
Ozark lake and the
crappie go ape-shit.
Chug it between
water hyacinths
at night on a Florida
river while bull frogs
bellow. You don't
want to think of the
deep blackness in the
mouth which will
rise beneath it.
It smells like blood
gone dead: a bucket
of shad gizzards,
waterlines of sludge-
choked rivers,
slowed to mud,
ringed with bones of carp.
But, God, it works!
Send it hissing
on a tippet out
over Montana streams,
and brown trout
will beach themselves.
To bluegill it is
that speck on the
skin of God.

To steelhead it comes
amazing and orange
under the face of the rain.
It will bring catfish
upstream like salmon.
A free sample is already
on its way to you.
(Batteries not included).

VASECTOMY

waiting for an hour alone
in the white room

naked from the waist down
clean flesh on clean sheets

polished steel and rubber tubes
behind reminiscences

of alcibiades on his*
lopping spree (would bogart

do this) and the doctor
in his cowboy boots

(did you hear the one
about the steer)

when wife had first child
she stood outside herself

listened to a distant scream
but this is different

even in the local numbness
my feet and neck converge

with the lifting of the cords
then fall back with the cutting

exhausted and sweating
I view my progeny

two segments like macaroni
stuck to the steel tray

*Alcibiades: A Greek who ran
around knocking the penises
off of statues.

103

BEARS ON THE WATER

Your sideways slap at a salmon
says more than we ever could.
Survival of the funnest:
that's what it boils down to
beyond all this tooth and claw.
Critics would say,
"This time the river has gone too far."
or "We came expecting drama;
we left feeling cheated
of the stage itself."
But you've got that soft shoe down
no matter what they say.
Your bumbling cubs in
that alder thicket
tug a sockeye
two ways at once.
They seem to have caught on.
There is no one way to do this thing.
You just do it till you're done.

ON THE BRIDGE

That night on the bridge a kid so black
he looked like a shadow on the waves
was fishing shrimp for drum. Cars slowed
when he hefted them silver under headlights,
over the rails and reflectors.
I stopped and watched for hours as shrimp
shot through the beam of his lantern
and his wet gunny sack twitched on pavement.
He was no shadow, though the way his line
sang that night seems darker to me
than the rivermouth was wide and deep.
His pole went down the way no drum
could move, so he dug his feet under
guard rails at first then had to run
for hours up and down the bridge,
reeling between the screams of his drag,
wearing one hand to blisters and the thumb
of the other a bloody nub. A bleary-eyed
boy in pajamas leaned from a van
and offered him a lavender Easter egg
found in a hunt at a mall that morning.
A man in a shirt with pictures of angel
fish offered him five dollars to
hold the blood-stained pole for a minute.
A Cuban woman in a flower print muu muu
tried to cut the line, but a surfer with
a bright cross chained to his neck held
her back until she ran off laughing.
Families red from the beach lined abutments
in bright suits under streetlamps reflecting
up like candles and fruit from the darker
water. But he'd take no help, even
from the man who offered a pistol.
And it was an odd crowd that followed him
silent to the end of the bridge and down
riprap where the jewfish bobbed up
into the colors and its mottled 400
pounds lay wide-eyed on concrete.

The kid called his brother
and they loaded it into a furniture
truck then drove toward the new light
coming up over the banks, the malls, the
revolving buckets of chicken, turning
the stars above us so far and clear
they threw the sky like their own distant
shadow over the whole ocean.

THE PEA-GRIFFS

Where I-35 runs north toward the Kansas border
my water pump went out, and I had to drive
ten miles west to a small town, radiator
howling and throwing steam like the ghost
of my old Ford, then dying slowly to
a whimper as I pulled into one of those
old stations that has pumps with rattling, spinning
balls. The attendant sent me across the street
to a cafe and asked me to return in three hours.
After miles of hard driving from Dallas, I
was still flying and the cafe, with its overhead
fan spinning, seemed to carry my mood.
I could easily have been dreaming until the woman
next to me jarred me with her voice like breaking
twigs, then her face, so concentric in wrinkles
that her nose could have been a stone thrown in.
"You seen the pea-griffs?" she asked. "The ones that
spun up out of the grass dead and moved like lopsided
bales on a piler?" I didn't answer, and I didn't
move. I was tired. I listened. "You know, it's weather.
It's the way the air stands still before a storm
that does it. Jus' like it happened the night
·Maty Balzer's memory trunk started rattlin'.
She'd put her husband's clothes in there the day
after he fell off the tractor and the discs went over
him. They was soaked with blood, but she jus' wadded
'em up an' throwed 'em in there where they stayed
for twenty years until that night. The storm
was comin' an' the wind-charger swung 'round
for no reason like it always did. Then
she heard it; the clothes in the trunk was movin'
an' when she run to open the darn thing,
they puffed up an' rose like the wind was blowin'
'cept there weren't no wind. Then somethin' like
a dust devil come into the yard, pickin' stuff
up 'til it was almost solid. Then it stopped
at the clothes, and darned if it didn't fill 'em up!

An' there was ol' Homer Balzer again. His face
was made out of lawn trimmin's and locust shells—
jus' like his hands. An' Maty wasn't scared
or nothin'—jus' like she'd been waitin' for this.
She took a deep breath an' tried to hug Homer,
but he flew into bits an' her arms went right through
him. When she stepped back he jus' sorta
settled together again. She was covered with husks,
thistles, an' grass so she knew he musta been real.
But when she tried to talk to him, he jus'
turned an' thumped off the porch an' across
the fields toward town. But that was jus' the first
of 'em. In town Lou Ella Pierson woke
to the sounda her dead sister's fox necklet
an' some of her other fur pieces rattlin'
off the hangers in the closet. It scared
the pee-waddin' outta her when it started
takin' shape from ol' costume jewelry an'
gum wrappers. When it got outside, grass
flew into it an' it looked jus' like Charlotte,
dead for fifteen years. There was never
no lossa love between the two
when she was alive, so Lou Ella throwed a
house-shoe at her, but insteada flyin' apart
it just sorta sucked onto her foot that was made
outa dry beakfast food. As Charlotte
rocked away down the street, Lou Ella
noticed dozensa others thumpin' an' rockin'
up to the park under the watertower.
Their relatives was followin' 'em, some
screamin' an' wailin' an' some jus' tryin' to keep
an eye on the darn things. Anyways,
as it turned out, there wasn't nothin' mysterious
about them pea-griffs. They wasn't alive.
It was jus' somethin' in that storm an' in
them dead people's clothes. "Cause when the rain
come, they jus' fell in heaps of rubbish
and clothes. The next mornin' we had one
heck of a time cleanin' up the park.
It was like somebody took a hay baler
an' run it cross-country then throwed all the bales
into the park, cut the twine, an' left
some ol' clothes to cover it all up.

I still got some flax that kinda looks
like the Reverend Adams hidden under
an old wagon box in my barn. Wanna
see it?'' Then a young man in a baseball
cap took her into a stream of sun and dustmotes
falling in from the street. She turned and said,
"In the barn." Back on the interstate I found
some pop music on KOMA and played
it loud all the way to Denver.

BLUEGRASS

Guitar is tired and
growing fat. He rears
his head then settles
back to the same old
tune. We all know
what he's trying to say,
for he's lived in our
village all his life.

Mandolin outguesses him,
seeing everything before-
hand. Under cool trees
in southern parks
he keeps it cooler after
dark and lives one string
at a time. He's only good
because he's young.

Fiddle is there all the
time whether we know it
or not. He wears the
weather's clothes and sings
for everyone but you.
Take him home to meet your
family and he's off to the
other end of your house.

Dobro got lost a long time
ago. That's obvious. And
he wears the strangest shoes
that he says are for dancing.
But you know different.
When he takes those long
vacations, you wish that
you could go along.

Bass never leaves and that
wouldn't be so bad except
he constantly talks about
how he never leaves. That
could get boring if it weren't
for his tremendous love of
birds. They fly happily in
and out of his losses.

Now banjo is standing there.
Now banjo is dancing.
Banjo banjo banjo banjo.
If he only knew how ridiculous
he is, but fame ruins
even the best of us. We
envy the fool.
The rich fool.

THE CRAPPIE FISHERMAN

He rows out on the lake at night.
Through his thin shirt the breeze
is cool then warm shifting from
lake—from shore. Under his lantern
the minnows collect—long tubelike
minnows that swirl at the gnats that
swirl at the lantern. The minnows
are translucent, so under the light
they are swimming skeletons. With
a wide square net he skims them
from the water. In his palm they
are opaque. The wind shifts again,
warm at the wet pop of the barb as
he slips it under the dorsal.

At first the minnow looks at home
again, dangled just below the surface,
as if the gnats and light were enough.
Then, slack released, it capsizes
and wriggles belly up into the deep green.
It lands and rights itself on the front
steps of a long submerged church, then
is hauled up to a man's height where it
rests dazed and twitching. A form
coalesces in the church door, also
at a man's height. Soon it is only
recognizable as an eye then a sideways
flash then it and the minnow are gone.

He is in the boat reeling. Under
the half moon his powder blue shirt
puffs up with the breeze and seems
separate from the bent neck, the furious
arm and hand. From the shore
it looks like an enormous water-bird
ruffling and preening against the dark.
When the man stops reeling, the wind
has shifted. It is cold again, he
puts on a coat as if the bird were
being swallowed by dark waves.

PURPLE WORM

I pop from the air-conditioned
Oldsmobile into the air-conditioned
mall with the stamp of Oklahoma
sun between. These two kinds
of weather put me in a world that
the skin doesn't know as I step up
to the aisle marked "fishing equipment"
and stare at lures with names opaque
as the glossed, reflective colors:
Mud-Bug, Hawg-Frawg, Mr. Twister.
The hum of shoppers and cool gusts
from vents above are saying these
names too. Everything seems to fit—
until I reach the plastic worms.
Here is something so close to life
against life, the red and white bobbers,
the orange day-glo marshmallows, the
catfish bait, secret in its red brown
behind glass, the rods like a bristling
field of dark weeds all wash into this
perfect lagoon where climate control
blows like curtains on a musty
lake-side resort at dusk. Walking
back to the car, I rip a worm with
a glowing orange tail from the pack
and shake it. Its air movement, its smell
in the air are telling me something about
the endlessly circling cars, the hamburger
and chicken joints flashing on the strip
toward home. My back yard slopes to a flood-
control project and the water backs up brown
in bushes and trees. Here the worm has my own
life on its line. The dark body, the orange
tail slide the mud bottom. I slip it
through an old channel I know from when
the project went dry (two fat water snakes
coiled there through last summer) and see
the boil of fins like cabbage leaves
and feed slack for seconds like minutes until it
stops and I strike.

The bass, its mouth a dark cave, breaks water
twenty yards out, and half the worm flies
back near my feet. With the orange tail gone,
it is dead and suddenly I feel the heat again.
The bass is fatter with its piece of warm plastic.
I am in here where it's cool.

CRICKETS

"Crickets for Sale" read
the dripping red letters,
and inside were large wire cages,
filled with the cheeping
whirl and scrawl.

She cupped out a dozen,
the woman with birds for hands,
and put them into a carton
like those used
for carry-out Chinese food.

All the way to the river,
we listened to them
without knowing it.

In the movie
a southern sheriff
rolled his flashlight's
beam over a swamp.
A cricket in the theater
stopped with those in
the illuminated grasses.

When I fell asleep,
the crickets awoke.
A summer of dreams
escaped me.

TURTLES

In Grandpa's garden I picked
up a terrapin. I was six
and serious as I stared down
at the gold and black of its shell.
It bit me on the stomach.
Grandma yelled. "It won't
let go until lightning flashes,"
but Father hit it with a flashlight,
the next best thing, and it let go.
At a pond in the pasture
Grandpa saw me drag a snapper
in on a cane pole.
It was almost three feet long,
and when I poked it,
it bit the pole in two.
Grandpa said, "Stand back,"
and cut its head off
then pried that from the hook.
When in the race the turtle won,
I'm sure jaws had something
to do with it.
And as for the civilization
that lived on one's back,
Grandpa, Grandma and the farm probably
had something to do with that too.

STUFFED FISH

for John Ashbery

They're always still wet, still
jumping in their prime, their mouths
ovalled for the kill, their gills
and fins flared red and cabbage green:
a bass in an attic, a trout in a
hamburger joint, a marlin in a
gas station, all arched as if their
oceans, streams and lakes would soon
appear below them; a bluegill
the size of a bean plate, stuck to a
plaque in a pastor's bathroom.
They will all swim the dusty air of our
leisure until their carded fins crack
and they become the Mona Lisas, the
glowing artifacts that future fingers
dust and caress from the rubble of
our failure. Under the shattered
beer mugs, under the formica and
toasters, under the crushed tvs and
shag carpets, will our stuffed fish
still shine, still swim in their
small miracle, wet from shallac and
sporting the pearly lacquers of those
small gods who hunched in their workshops
with scalpels and brushes, alum and
cardboard and thought FISH until they
had devised a little lesson for
those who would treat fish casually:
a lesson where the teacher becomes
deception, as if art were a naive kid
walking into a tackle shop and buying
a lure that looks like Christ himself,
a lesson where the shopkeeper's catlike
eyes gleam with the words *Good luck son*
and eternity turns out to be a horrible
black fish that takes the plug?

THE FLOUNDER

I will give you three wishes he said
but there was a storm and the sea
was a gray wall and I could not hear
very well. Besides, my family was hungry.
That night as we sat at the table
my youngest boy would not eat because
of the odd color, the huge eye.
My eldest picked at it driven through
revulsion by hunger.
My wife ate it out of obligation.
I ate the most as they rolled
boiled potatoes onto their plates
and watched me askance.

I told them what I had thought I heard
in the wind and they stared down at
gray skin on white meat.
The wind blew the ocean against
the rocks and then our cottage.
I had always given them nothing but meat.

This thing on the plate in front of us
was a shredded possibility
more vacant than the words
I heard hissing over its gills
into the wind.

Over the village that night,
a large cloud passed, spotted
with moonlight then blazing in one
place where the moon formed an eye.

Come out and look, I said to my family.
It is not too late.
Something is happening.
But they stayed inside playing
the small games that always
carried them through the winter.

ABOUT THE AUTHOR

Greg Keeler is a professor of English at Montana State University in Bozeman, Montana, where he lives with his wife, Judy, and their boys, Chris and Max. Besides teaching and writing, Keeler composes and sings satirical lyrics about the West; and through Earth First! Music, he has released three tapes of his songs. His poems have appeared in *Gray's Sporting Journal, Prairie Schooner, Cutbank, Berkeley Poetry Review, Northern Lights,* and various anthologies, as well as in two previous Confluence Press collections. Several of the poems in *American Falls* recall Keeler's childhood with his family and his father, Clinton Keeler, who was also an English professor, a poet, and a fisherman.